WHITE NOISE LULLABY

POEMS

AMY MILLER

CYCLONE PRESS

ASHLAND, OREGON

© 2015 by Amy Miller

White Noise Lullaby
ISBN 978-0-9839274-5-7
First printing: September 2015

Cover image: *Lunar Corona* by Wing-Chi Poon
Author photo by Megan Boone

Cyclone Press

Ashland, Oregon
writers-island.blogspot.com

Contents

Monte Sereno	5
Afterlife	6
Tournament	7
Bike Path	8
A Lullaby	11
Seven Climaxes	12
A Table in Space	14
Thinking about My Brother while Making Coffee	16
This Body	17
The Poet Laureate in the Laundromat	18
Six Objects That Are Mine and One That Isn't	19
The Collage Kids	20
Ten Caltrain Haikus	21
For Those Who Would Kill Chickens	23
Angel for Larry	25
Rhosymedre	26
The Trouble with New England Girls	27
A Dream That Must Have Been My Father's	29
"Worried Man Blues"	30
Acknowledgments	32
Author bio	33

Monte Sereno

When I had two spoons,
the kitchen was a bathroom,
the closet was a cupboard.
The fridge tuned its fork,
lonesome in the shed. In rain,
the roses splayed and bricks
forgot their mortar. I had

one knife, a saw,
and somebody's old hammer. Rats
made feast of the rafters,
frost brought the moon
and the brown moving
shapes of coyotes. I had
two bowls and a steel
teapot ticking,
ticking on the warm
burner in the dark.

Afterlife

My sister asks
if I think we'll see our mother again.
I'm thinking I'll see her Sunday,
play two-handed bridge, sit
on the couch for as long as it takes her
to tell me Dad is driving her crazy,
that she's throwing up
even the liquid food now.

My sister means the afterlife,
her high, bright country club
where everyone sheds
their skin and forgets
what it means to be angry.
There's no spit
in heaven, I think, no fight,
and how does everyone find each other?
How can we sit down
to that intelligent picnic?

I tell my sister I don't know,
that I'm doing my seeing now.
I know exactly how to shame her.

Tournament

How I wanted to keep up. How everything tasted so sweet: the
brandy, the beer. Where we started—Scrabble in the kitchen
while Mom poured peanuts into bridge bowls and summer
drummed on the night screen, warm wings of air. How the
bridge ladies came, talked of the roads and the worlds of their
houses, a chorus from another room when Mom stepped
into the middle, the winner and still champ-een but humble,
offering coffee and milk. She beat them every week. She did not
tell me this, but I knew the incandescence of that block on the
calendar, how she would not love a thing she could not square
up to and belt out of the park into the sky with all its old bear
and bull stories and men marching around with swords and
hunting dogs. How she led even the dimmest partner to bid a
shark's hand—she would not bother with the talk if the math
and strategy didn't burn bright holes in the table. How the
house billowed with her thinking, my sister and I slipping out
and hitting the store for Heineken Darks, my sister's Beetle with
the rusted floor, her two-story house across town (take a right
at the Flaming O). And how the night was a pulse, how we
pulled that glorious dull into our mouths, that sweet, forgiving
dumb. How we wasted that night on talk we'll never remember.
How my sister kept on drinking—the wizard power of her
body, changing brandy into blood, lighting every cigarette with
a welder's precision. How she drove me home late, my key
like the voice of a mouse in the lock. How I lost—the game
of keeping up and every fleck of food I had. How my sister
mopped the floor with the warm, damp mass of me. How even
her Scrabble words were seven letters, bonus points, so far ahead
she might as well have been a star in her own unfathomable sky.

Bike Path

half of us are sure
who did it
        sun-stained face
        half feral   where
        would he hide
        a blade that big
        winter   in his coat

when the doorbell
                rings
I have to think
        where
is that wreath
does it block
the hole
I would see him through
        a voice
says clear
says loud
        it's me
        it's Mary
        your neighbor

in the grocery store
a man
so kind
        the cashier
        blushes as she takes
        his money
his face
        flushed
from walking
or wind

        a killer
        eats too
        what would he buy?

outside, in the dark
        our bags   our meat
        our apples and razors
we could hide
and do anything
even
watch each other   close
from behind
        windshield glass

somebody hacked
        the trees up good
for days
        they walked the path
in rubber gloves
        pressing plaster
        in cut marks

paper tiger
        in the neighbor's
        window   wasn't
        there
before   beautiful
        way to not
                see
        not see
                in

walking home
        he must

    have heard
                        something
    behind him

    I loved
        that trail
    how it winds
        past the little
    campfire spot
      out
        into oaks
        and madrones
    I might have
        met a dog
        a man
        said hello
        kept walking

A Lullaby

Sleep now. The city
you were building in your head,
its shouting and conveyances,
its strikers and unhelpful signs,
its cops with their stern citations,
rest. Rest the piteous call
from your sister and the words
you boiled in the pot
all day.

       Somewhere
deer fatten in a sudden
thaw. A lake floats hundreds
of Russians in bathing suits.
And your dreams—no one can take
those wild paintings
and unbelievable music,
or your lashes dropping
their feathers, or the factory
of your own lungs,
quietly working into the night.

Seven Climaxes

buzzer-
beater   thousands
leap up   arms
bare, thrown
high   screaming
I tell you
they were screaming

this story just
escalated but see
it's actually the climax
did you think
there was more?

I have to have
that jacket   it would make
even me think
I knew
what I was doing

I helped
the airplane climb
willed it up
from the fiery earth
with my crossed fingers
and a fervent
engineer's prayer

from this hill the city
stretches out,
bends the eye's perspective by
ramping up two other hills
due north, a bridge tower
rising at the back
like an ornament
in its hair

when we talk
about release
we are talking
about death
all this living
the buildup

after, we ate
an apple I split
with a knife
your two quarters
with the heart carved
out   mine just
the same

A Table in Space

I love my big,
loud friend
who mauls waiters
and always orders
the jumbo beer,
anything called "fat" or "ass,"
who stabs his steak
with no remorse
for yesterday's slaughter,
for nitrates and oil
rushing to the fire sale
of his heart.

I love the way
I sometimes wish
I could turn down
the volume knob
under his shirt,
the big one in the middle
among the dials for dirty jokes,
the switch
for sudden tenderness,
the gauge
with this father's death
at the red end
where the needle pins.

The way the evening
seems like a month,
the way the roof
leans over him,

listening for his praise—
his pool of gravity
bends the table,
bottles docked
next to the spaceships
of our bodies, my ears
turning their small dishes
toward him,
sifting out of the night
his one strong signal.

Thinking about My Brother While Making Coffee

Thinking about that girl
he met in a Paris museum.
He took her home to wherever
home was, his or hers,
cramped flat
in an immigrant *arrondissement*.
He didn't know, he said,
until later that it was
his birthday, as if
the universe were a much
cooler family. The coffee
was better, the streets
more artfully curved, so unlike
the pinched suburban corners
we knew. This was before
he changed his name. I keep
going back to the coffee in Paris,
the way they bring it out
in its own drip cone,
how it must have smelled
like the future,
how the girl in the museum
must have looked to him,
her hair falling like cedars
on the Pyrenees of her brow, and,
over her shoulder,
a painting—
a shimmering band
broken free and flying
over the old ground.

This Body

pulls a little
to the left, starts slowly
some mornings after late
nights sorting broken

from rust. It swerves
from calling
anyone useless unless
it's a good joke or just

the metal truth,
the gut (in all
its glorious
schematics) turning

fitfully, fretfully over.
That is to say, this body
knows its holy-
shit collisions,

faint scrapes
and sideswipes (lucky
near and total quarter-
panel crumples),

                      burns
the ember of a touch
forever in its small
efficient tank.

The Poet Laureate in the Laundromat

for Lawson Fusao Inada

He stands to watch the comforter
hug and unhug itself
as the dryer muscles on and hums
its white noise lullaby.
Even in the warm, overbright room,
he wears a leather jacket, hands
pushed deep in the pockets. Music,
perhaps, is what he hears
in the tinning and rumble,
notes dopplered to a shriek. Or poems,
spinning and powered
by their own unseen magnets.
He is not writing this down.
It washes over, river
and color and metal. But sometimes
something catches—
there, you can see—
he tilts his head, surprised.

Six Objects That Are Mine and One That Isn't

After a day of doctors and work
and money and even
the painstaking steering
to not hit that jerk
in the parking garage,
the soft hermetic
closing of my door sounds
like an army of angels
laying down their guns.
And my kitchen, the last
brown shards of sunset
sliding their blades
across the cabinets,
suddenly is paradise, the faucet
playing small creek music
as six objects on the sill—
two horses, a soapstone god,
the clock, the cup and bowl—
hold quiet court with the one
I'll never fully own, the plant
turning its panels to light
and mining a life
from its fistful of soil.

The Collage Kids

drive up the price of magazines
and gum spirits. Crackle,
crackle all night and mutter
headlines behind that paper
wall. Unnatural bodies
and heads press together, shellac
defiling hair, pasted, planted
upside down, cropped close,
the little restless birds
of their scissors chirping.

Ten Caltrain Haikus

At Vince's Shellfish
men driving mini-forklifts
levitate white bins.

Pickups in the mud.
Two workers in orange vests
clutching coffee cups.

The Brisbane marshpond
furrows with a pre-storm wind.
Birds ride the ripples.

Old Candlestick Park.
Dark towers veining the fog.
No one plays today.

Pigeons flying out
from under the overpass
land on a loft roof.

The conductor taps
his ring against the railing.
Who is lost in thought?

Twenty-Second Street.
Birds flutter in an old tree
hung with plastic bags.

The fresh graffiti
says "C3PO is gay."
A homeless man smokes.

The Korean church
shows its spire to the sky:
vertical language.

In the long tunnel,
I always expect to see
Oz when we come out.

For Those Who Would Kill Chickens

I wish I could show you
how we saved him. Named him
Steven, stupid name
for a chicken, but
when he wandered
out from the woods,
black sheen hooked
with leaves and the crazy
red rubber of his comb,
we had to call him
something. I thought
Lucky after a horse
stomped him so hard—
caught in the corral
like a mouse in traffic—
then maybe Rip
when he tucked his head
in the elbow of the foreman's
wife and fell asleep
in her arms. *Steven*,
she whispered—who knows,
some baby or a friend
long gone—and it stuck.
I could show you
my sandwiches he pulverized,
his crooked Jagger dance
on the paddock's dusty stage,
how each of us came
to grudgingly help
this alien flown from some
coop, how a thing
like that takes root

on a shelf in a dark
tack room, settling
on an overshirt you meant
to take home that now
is sacrificed—no matter—
to this thing you've named,
that needs you. Each night
we closed and locked
that door against whatever
was out there
that hadn't yet learned
his name or the iridescence
of his weak and perfect wings.

Angel for Larry

When his angel came,
she showed up in Broadway-red hair
and driving a white Fiesta,
the trunk held shut
with bungee cords.
It barely fit his wheelchair,
but she pushed him

through the wind-flapped farmer's market,
down the tumbling creek
with the asphalt path,
the old trees green-bearded
and nodding as he passed.
Her wings were so transparent

that he never saw them
lift him up in the morning,
barely wondered at the days
when all he needed was his walker
that she unfolded with a hip
and a hand, the other
levitating him out
of his breakfast chair.

Just now she took him to the park
like a healer at a tent revival
with no crowd to watch her
working the elements, gravity
and time suspended while she knelt
before him on the impossible grass
he had to walk to get there,
a shaft of sun
splitting the shadowed hills,
igniting her hair
like a small tree burning.

Rhosymedre

We were so unlovely. We butchered our bows
on the crescendos. Our fingers pawed
the backward strings, drunken pizzicatos
clattering the lanes of a quiet town.
The hymn broke through,

violas parting wild ground
like the plows of heavy horses,
turning up a skeleton of sharped C's
and switchback scales. It looked

so simple—whole measures
on a single string—but then the violence
of pursuit, cellos bucking their separate arcs,
half the violins stalling in air.
Still, I heard it hum

the phrases of my middle ear,
the theme of my short drive home,
love's face gone from the window
of the night café, a dog's bright collar
dancing a diminuendo in the crosswalk.

*"Rhosymedre" ("Lovely"): a song adapted by
Ralph Vaughan Williams for "Three Preludes on
Welsh Hymn Tunes," now a staple of small orchestras*

The Trouble With New England Girls

They think the moon rises
and sets. They speak English
as if English were their one
true tongue.
              They have hair
and they have teeth
and sometimes they wear
bad sweaters
                  missing a button.
They live in houses
with mothers for the most part,
brothers, dads,
                dogs
patrolling the yards.
Sometimes they drive out
under the moon.
Sometimes they get pregnant
and drive to New Jersey
and sometimes
                they come back
married and quiet,
or quiet and alone.
And sometimes they steal
the bus fare
              to get there
and back.
              Sometimes
they feel the ocean
pinning the wrists of the land,

the stars
looking down, unblinking,
                            the moon
with its third-degree light
pounding the truth
right out of them.
                    They wish
they were Baja girls
shimmering on a beach,
not a bus
or sweater
in sight,
and the moon
                  far up there
                  in the untouchable dark
where it belongs.

A Dream That Must Have Been My Father's

One saw was mine—
silver and sharp-toothed,
a hand-carved handle I lifted
to the peg. Up
in the rafters' dark,
I saw another—
Who leaves beauty behind?—
hanging from a hole
in its venerable blade.
I lifted it down,
and I swear
it purred like a fed cat,
my whole shop humming.
Nails in their boxes
waited to rain like arrows
on an unsure enemy.
The rope I'd coiled
around one arm
lay like a sleepy centerfold.
The room itself was metaphor,
the firebox of my dreaming.
No one came
to speak to me there,
no one sat tall
on the high stool,
watching the sawdust land
like snow
on the cold, clean floor.

"Worried Man Blues"

Halfway through the song,
the dog bumped
his big black
pit bull head
against my leg
and I stopped—
small rest
between the banjo
and the guitar player
who never sits down.
My ragged chords caught
their breath, the bow
dropped and turned
and pressed against the fiddle,
freeing one hand
to hold that warm,
soft ear
with its own dark valley
of music.

Acknowledgments

Grateful acknowledgment is made to the following journals and anthologies, in which many of these poems (some in earlier versions) appeared:

Bird's Thumb: "Seven Climaxes"

Camas: "Monte Sereno"

Crab Orchard Review: "The Trouble with New England Girls"

Elohi Gadugi: "Thinking about My Brother while Making Coffee"

Gold Man Review: "A Table in Space," "Rhosymedre," "'Worried Man Blues'"

The Knotted Bond: Oregon Poets Speak of Their Sisters: "Afterlife"

Nimrod: "Angel for Larry," "A Dream That Must Have Been My Father's," "This Body," "Tournament"

Rattle: "For Those Who Would Kill Chickens," "A Lullaby"

Right Hand Pointing: "The Collage Kids"

Spillway: "The Poet Laureate in the Laundromat," "Six Objects That Are Mine and One That Isn't"

Whistle Stop: "Ten Caltrain Haikus"

ZYZZYVA: "Bike Path"

Thanks also to the following writers whose workshop help on these poems was invaluable: Linda Barnes, Jonah Bornstein, Jeannette Cappella, Angela Howe Decker, Steve Dieffenbacher, Sallie Ehrman, Susan Clayton Goldner, Marcy Greene, Kim Hamilton, Amy MacLennan, Joan Peterson, Liz Robinson, Jay Schroder, Pepper Trail, Petra Whitaker, and Patty Wixon.

Raised in northern California and western Massachusetts, Amy Miller worked as a ranch hand, electronic assembler, photographer's assistant, bookkeeper, and ad salesperson before settling into a career as an editor and print project manager. Her writing has appeared in *Many Mountains Moving*, *Nimrod*, *Rattle*, *Willow Springs*, *ZYZZYVA*, *Fine Gardening*, *Asimov's Science Fiction*, *The Writer's Journal*, and *The Poet's Market,* and anthologies such as *What the River Brings: Oregon River Poems* and *Clash by Night: A London Calling Anthology*. She won the Cultural Center of Cape Cod National Poetry Competition, judged by Tony Hoagland, the *Whiskey Island* Poetry Prize, the Poetry Storehouse videopoem prize, the Kay Snow Award, and the *Cloudbank* Award, and has been a finalist for the Pablo Neruda Prize, the 49th Parallel Award, and *A Prairie Home Companion*'s Sonnet Contest. Other chapbooks include *Rough House* (White Knuckle Press, 2016), *In the Hand*, *Tea Before Questions*, and *The Mechanics of the Rescue*. She lives in Ashland, Oregon, where she is the poetry editor of the NPR listening guide *Jefferson Monthly*, works as the publications project manager for the Oregon Shakespeare Festival, and blogs at writers-island.blogspot.com.

www.ingramcontent.com/pod-product-compliance
Lightning Source LLC
Chambersburg PA
CBHW031440040426
42444CB00006B/898